BOOK OF PARTY GAMES

Compiled by **Matt Kavet**

Illustrated by **Jerry King & Martin Riskin**
Layout by **CoffeyCup Productions**

Boston America Corp.
125 Walnut Street, Watertown, MA 02172   617-923-1111 Fax: 617-923-8839

INTRODUCTION

You want to have a good party? Soitenly. So, grab yourself a couple of willing goils or if you are of the feminine gender a couple of good looking guys like us. Then pick out a few games from this here book that have been poysunally selected by the three of us. Well, maybe 2 of us: Curly don't read so good. Your party is guaranteed to be successful and full of rambunctious fun.

This book may not have too many namby pamby parlor games but it's full of raucous, sexy, sloppy, boisterous ones that will bring the cops and keep up your neighbors. Okay, knuckleheads, enough of reading stupid introductions. Your guests are arriving soon so pick out a few games to start with.

FORFEITS

You'll see this word throughout our book. It's a penalty for the loser; kind of the opposite of a prize for the winner which you can also do should you have lots of good prizes around. Forfeits can be something like finishing your drink (but we are soitenly not suggesting you use alcoholic beverages that could make a poysun drunk) or kissing people which is always nice especially with the opposite sex and if everyone brushes their teeth.

You can use the removal of articles of clothing, making speeches, having a player tell the 5 best and worst features about themselves or those of a friend or spouse. Forfeits can be washing the dishes, acting as bartender, running the next game or doing a ballet. Use your imagination. You ain't a bunch of dummies.

BALLOON BUST

"Sometimes when we play *Balloon Bust* the guys get a little carried away".

BALLOON BUST

This is a dumb game but a good noisy starter that gets a little body contact going even if it's with your own spouse or date.

Each couple places a large balloon between themselves and at the start tries to break it using body pressure alone. Last to break their balloons pays a forfeit.

STRIP POKER

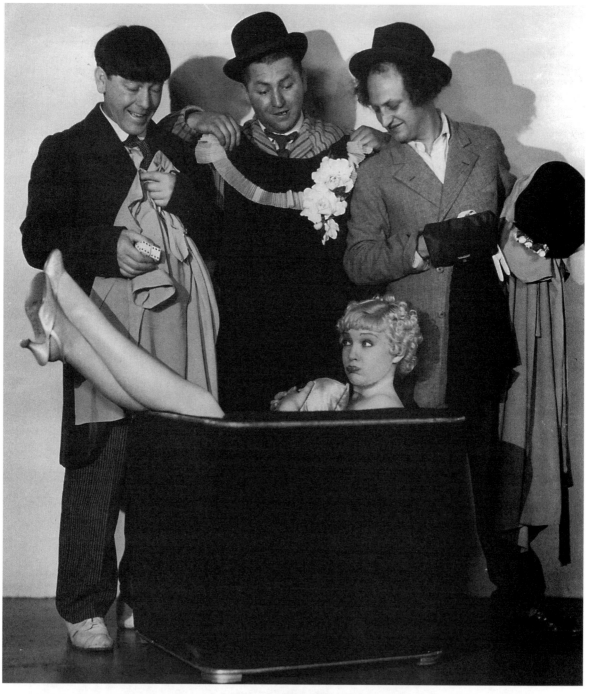

Moe is willing to switch to dice to give this lovely lady a chance to win back her duds.

STRIP POKER

If you can ever find some good looking goils, like the one on the left, willing to play strip poker be sure to invite the three of us. Everyone knows how to play strip poker but playing it as a team adds more fun and makes it easier to get the shy people at your party to participate. After all, strip poker with a bunch of hairy guys ain't so much fun.

Divide your guests into an even number of teams. The teams can be girls versus guys or mixed. Each team picks one member to play for them. Rules are the same as for regular poker only all the team members' clothes are bet instead of money or chips. Each article of clothing counts as one unit and don't allow people to cheat by using shoelaces, handkerchiefs, jewelry and the like.

DRESS ME UP
DRESS ME DOWN

"Whaddayah mean this is a Ladies Room?"

DRESS ME UP
DRESS ME DOWN

This one is great for all your friends who are closet cross dressers.

Gather various pieces of hand luggage; suitcases, gym bags, briefcases, even shopping or bowling bags will work. You'll need one per couple and fill each with a workable but outrageous outfit of goil and boy clothes. The clothing can be as risqué or sedate as your crowd feels comfortable with. Our crowd will wear almost anything. The couples pick a suitcase and retire to different rooms. They dress up using the various outfits found in their bags and as little else as possible. When all return the group votes on the winners and losers.

BLIND MAN'S FEEL

Be careful if you are playing this game with people who are sensitive about where you touch them or their wives.

BLIND MAN'S FEEL

This game can be really racy or much more mild than it sounds in case your guests are a little timid. The goils all go to another room and are carefully blindfolded. They are brought back, one at a time, and try to identify the boys by feeling only one agreed upon part of their bodies. Neck, head, waist, thigh, or whatever you can get away with all are good. The boys being felt shouldn't giggle and the woman who identifies the most correctly wins. The loser can pay a forfeit. Next you can switch around and have the guys try, provided they behave like gentlemen, or you can do both sexes together. Hey, it's your party.

"I HAVE AN IDEA. LET'S PLAY BLIND MAN'S FEEL!"

WIND BAG

Curly is an expert at this game and practices by blowing golf balls through a hose.

WIND BAG

This is an easy game to get everyone involved with, even the wallflowers you're sorry you invited. Guests sit or kneel in a circle holding the edges of a sheet or table cloth. A feather is placed in the middle. Everyone blows trying to keep the feather away from themselves. If you are touched by the feather you must carry out a forfeit as described on Page 3 which you probably didn't read and the game continues.

A similar game can be played by teams lining up on either side of a table and trying to blow a Ping Pong ball off the opposite team's edge.

GROUP GROPE

Everyone seems to be groping in this corner of the room.

GROUP GROPE

Everyone is blindfolded or all lights are turned off if the room can be made totally dark.

Players try to find their date or spouse by "feeling around." No talking is allowed but when a couple thinks they've found each other they can whisper each other's name. Once the couples are hooked up blindfolds can be removed to enjoy the antics of the people still groping.

SPARE MY LIFE

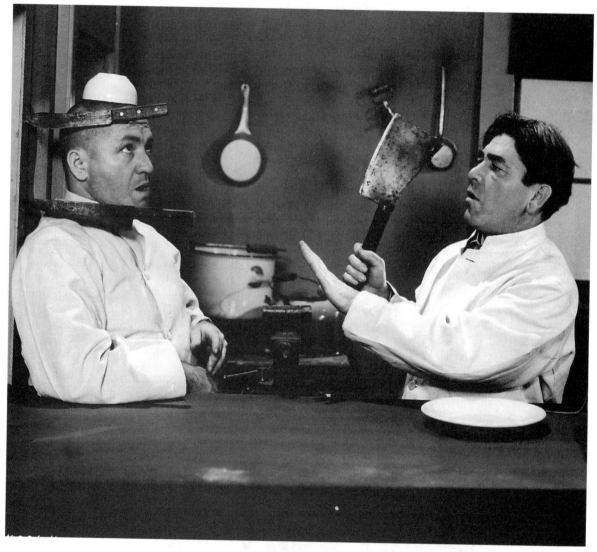

Moe isn't trying to kill Curly; he's just teaching him a new trick.

SPARE MY LIFE

Tell your guests to pretend that they are all floating in the North Atlantic in a leaky lifeboat after their ship has sunk. The water is starting to slosh over the gunnels and the ocean is shark infested. To prevent the boat from sinking one guest must be thrown overboard to lighten the load and save the others. Each occupant of the lifeboat is allowed a one minute plea to explain why she or he should be allowed to remain. The player might claim he or she is enormously wealthy and will pay each survivor a million dollars or is a famous physicist about to complete work on an amazing new energy source that will be of incalculable benefit to mankind or a widowed mother of 6 small children. You get the idea. Guests vote on the stories to decide who is most expendable and the player who "gets thrown overboard" pays a forfeit.

PARTY LINE

"Yeah, I can hear fine now."

PARTY LINE

One guest makes up a ribald story perhaps about another guest. It should be short, maybe 50 words and should be ridiculous and complicated. That shouldn't be hard for you knuckleheads.

Players sit in a line or circle and the first reads the story and then whispers it to the next player in line. The story is whispered down the line like the old "telephone" game you played as a kid. The final player tells what she or he heard, which to the guffaws of all, is compared to the written version.

On A Roll

" You expect me to measure these classy dames with
a roll of toilet paper?"

On A Roll

This is an easy game that even reluctant game players will enjoy. As guests arrive, hold out a roll of toilet paper and asks each guest to tear off whatever length of toilet paper they think they will need. You don't have to explain what they might need it for, unless it's that kind of party. You might want to say, "We're a little short of toilet paper tonight, and we want to make sure we don't run out."

At some point during the party, gather all the guests together and then measure the guest of honor's bust line or waist line (or whatever part the crowd decides to measure.) The guest who has the strip of toilet paper closest to that length wins a prize.

NAME YOUR POISON

"Hey, this ain't apple juice".

NAME YOUR POISON

Most people haven't the slightest idea what kind of alcohol they drink. Oh, maybe they can tell the difference between gin and scotch, but not between Johnny Walker Red and Black.

To play this game, you simply line up shot glasses full of 10 or 15 different kinds of liquor to see just how many can be identified by your party guests. If nothing else, it will let you know when to switch to the cheap booze. The rules are simple: no tasting is allowed and players must rely on sense of smell only. (If guests are really having a hard time naming the liquor, you could modify the rules and let everyone put a drop on the tip of their tongue.) The one who can identify the most shots correctly is the winner, whose reward should be to finish his or her favorite. If few people can identify anything, as we suspect, it will give you an idea of how much money you can save on liquor at your next party.

SARDINE

Sardine is a snugly game that makes Moe and Curly
jealous when they can't find the sardine.

SARDINE

This is a great game to get your party guests bonding together - in one great big squirmy heap.

Before the party, cut some blank paper into as many strips as there are guests. Write the letter S on one slip and leave the rest blank, then put all the slips in a bowl. The player to pick the S is the Sardine. All the players start out in the same room and the lights throughout the whole house are turned off. The Sardine finds a suitable hiding place and stays there motionless. As the other players encounter each other in the dark, they ask each other, "Are you the Sardine?" If the answer is "No," they keep searching. If the answer is "Yes," that player joins the Sardine in the secret hiding place, snuggling as close to him as possible. As more and more players find the Sardine and join him, the more cramped the hiding place becomes and inevitably the guests start giggling. After a set time limit, the few pathetic shmucks who have apparently lost most of their faculties, including their hearing and sense of direction, must carry out a forfeit.

HATS OFF MUSICAL CHAIRS

"Why do we always get stuck providing the music instead of playing with the goils?"

HATS OFF MUSICAL CHAIRS

This is another variation of the old stand by, Musical Chairs. It's a lot of fun to play if your guests don't mind leaving your party looking like they've had a really bad hair day.

All you have to do is provide a bunch of funky hats ranging from Easter bonnets to knit ski hats to baseball caps. A toupee or wig adds to the fun, too. Someone is in charge of starting and stopping the music and all the other guests stand in a circle. Every guest but one wears a hat. When the music starts, players grab the hat off their neighbor's head and put it on their own and continue until the music stops. The person left without a hat is out.

COMING UP SHORT

"Now where did youse guys hide the yarn?"

COMING UP SHORT

Before the party, hide 40 - 60 different lengths of colorful yarn around the house. After guests arrive and they are divided into teams, instruct them to search for the yarn. You could color coordinate each group and have teams look for certain colors, or just let the teams collect any color yarn they happen upon for about 15 minutes.

After guests frantically turn over couch cushions and dig through your potted plants and linen closet to uncover the yarn, have each team tie together all the yarn they have gathered. The team with the longest string wins.

WHISTLE WHILE YOU WORK

Washing your crackers down with seltzer is cheating.

WHISTLE WHILE YOU WORK

This is a fun one for dummies who talk with their mouth full and don't mind making a mess. The players are divided into two teams and line up facing each other. When you say "Go," the first person in each line shovels three salty crackers into his mouth. When he's finished eating them, he whistles the first line of a popular song. When that player is done whistling, the next player in line eats three crackers and whistles the second line of the song. Play continues down the line until everyone has had a turn. The first team to finish wins.

"IT'S THE BEST PARTY WE'VE EVER BEEN TO."

GLOVES AND SOCKS

This photo has nothing to do with the *Gloves and Socks* game but it soitenly shows the kind of *goils* we like at our parties.

GLOVES AND SOCKS

This game is silly but it gets everyone in a light, fun mood almost instantly. Divide the guests into two groups and ask all the members of one group to put on mismatched pairs of gloves. The bigger and more awkward the gloves the better. They can range from ski gloves to oven mitts to boxing gloves, if you've got them. The first group sits in circle facing inward wearing their crazy gloves. In the center of the circle is a huge pile of various socks from sheer knee highs to heavy woolen socks to tiny peds with pom pons on the heel. Just before play begins, the spectator group ties blindfolds on every player. The object of the game is for players to put on as many socks as possible while wearing the gloves and blindfolds. The group of guest spectators for the first round will have as much fun as the participants just by watching them go at it.

Pass The Buck

You can keep the bucks if we can keep the dames.

Pass The Buck

Remember the old game where players passed oranges held under their chins or passed lifesavers on toothpicks held between their teeth? Well, this one is more fun.

Guests should line up man-woman-man-woman in as many rows as possible with at least six people per row. The object of the game is to pass a dollar bill from person to person in the row as quickly as possible. The catch is that the dollar bill is held between each player's knees. Players are apt to crack up while trying to contort into the best position possible for passing the bills. The first team to pass the dollar from the beginning to the end of the line wins. Their prize is keeping all the dollars.

SPOONS

"The fun part about *Spoons* is getting real close, n'yuk, n'yuk, n'yuk."

SPOONS

Guests must line up in two rows in man-woman-man-woman order. The first person in each line is given a cold spoon with about four yards of string or yarn attached. At your command, she must drop the spoon **DOWN** her shirt and feed it out through her skirt or pant leg. The game's lots more fun if the spoon's against a person's skin. If necessary, the next player in line can lend a helping hand. Then he must take the spoon and string it **UP** through his clothes starting at the lowest point of entry so it comes out at the collar of his shirt. The spoon must be strung through the whole line of players in an up-down-down-up sequence until everyone is threaded together. When the last person has finished, everyone stands shoulder to shoulder as closely together as possible. The string is then cut at the place of entry on the first person in the row. The last person in the row pulls the string out and the team with the shortest string is the winner.

RISQUÉ CHARADES

First, assemble a group of fun loving, open minded friends. This is the only hard part. Most people already know how to play Charades so you really don't have to bother reading these instructions - just plunge right in.

RISQUÉ CHARADES

In case you've been a hermit all your life or you're a newcomer to this country here is the general idea: The group is divided into two teams. One team picks a phrase (perhaps from the risqué list provided below) and whispers it or writes it out for one opposing team member. That person becomes the "Actor" and may not show or tell the phrase to his or her teammates, but must act out the words using pantomime. The teammates try to guess the phrase within a given time limit.

That's all there is to it and you're allowed to make up your own rules – I'm not your mother, after all. Both teams can play at the same time which leads to a very exciting game but one in which the players miss the fun of watching the other actors struggle with their phrase. Just do what's the most fun for you. This is a party after all, not a final exam.

If you've never played before, these tips may help:
1. To indicate the length of the phrase, the actor holds up as many fingers as there are words.
2. To indicate the number of syllables in a word, the actor holds out his arm and places as many fingers as there are syllables on his forearm.
3. To indicate that a little word or conjunction like a, an, and, but, it, to, if, or the, is in the phrase, the actor makes a sign for "tiny" by holding up her thumb and forefinger with only a small space between them. All the teammates yell out little words until someone guesses the right one.
4. To indicate "sounds like" the actor cups his hand behind his ear.

Winning The Game
A team wins by guessing the phrase in the shortest time or by getting the best overall time for several rounds of play. You decide who wins. After all, you are all grown ups – otherwise, you shouldn't be playing this game.

MURDER

"I charge you with the heinous crime of *Murder*."

Cut a sheet of paper into as many slips as there are
guests. Mark one slip with an **X** and another with a **D**.
Leave the rest of the slips blank and put them all,
folded, into a bowl for guests to draw from. The player
who draws the **X** is the Murderer and the player to
draw the **D** is the detective. The murderer keeps her or
his identity secret and all slips are put back into the
bowl. The detective leaves the room and the lights are

MURDER

switched off. The rest of the players move around the room in the dark, and when the murderer puts her hands on the victim, that player must scream and fall to the floor. Then the lights are switched on and the detective is called back into the room to start the super sleuthing. The detective may ask as many questions as he wants and all players except the murderer must answer truthfully. The detective gets only one guess and when he thinks he knows who the murderer is he says, "I charge you (suspect's name) with the heinous crime of murdering (victim's name)." If the guess is correct, the murderer must admit her guilt. Like most adventurous and exciting pastimes, Murder is best played in the dark! But, if you are pathetic enough to have a party during daylight hours, there is another murderously fun game to play called "Wink," that must be played in the light.

Pull as many cards from a deck of playing cards as there are guests at the party. One of the cards must be the Ace of Spades. Every player picks a card and the one who draws the Ace is deemed the Murderer. He must "kill" his victims by winking at them, but he must be quick and clever about it so no one else sees him do the terrible deed. The rest of the players look all around the room at each other trying to figure out the identity of the murderer. The object of the game is for the murderer to kill off everyone without being discovered. When victims are "killed," they should wait a few seconds before they wail their dying breath so they don't give the murderer away. The person to catch the murderer in the act is the winner, but if someone falsely accuses another player, the penalty is instant death.

TASTE TEST

" You're supposed to taste it knucklehead, not swim in it."

TASTE TEST

If you can't deal with serving dainty finger sandwiches or escargot at your party, play this game and you can skip the hors d'oeuvres all together.

"I, FOR ONE, PREFER HORS D'OEUVRES TO ANY STUPID GAME."

Remove the labels from 10 or 15 jars of baby food and tape a code on each jar so you alone can identify the contents. Put the jars on a tray with a supply of those little plastic tasting spoons you get at ice cream shops. (No I don't know where to buy them.) Players dip a clean spoon in each jar and taste the contents trying to guess what it is. Players with the most correct answers do NOT have to finish the leftover strained carrots or spinach and liver mix.

BEST GUESS

"Hey Curly, just count the stuff in the bowl don't eat it."

BEST GUESS

Before guests arrive, fill a glass jar or clear bowl with a predetermined number of jellybeans, candy corn, peanuts, M&M's® or some other desirable foodstuff.

Guests simply fill out slips of paper with their "guesstimate" of the total number of objects in the jar. The player who guesses closest to the actual amount is the winner and gets to take home the jar full of goodies or distribute select quantities to their friends.

Sign My Check

Curly can't sign so good after washing and drying his hands.

Sign My Check

Every guest puts a brown paper bag over the hand they write with. Then they go around the room and ask the other guests to autograph their bag. Of course, the others will also have their writing hands covered so they must sign their John Hancock with the wrong hand.

This can result in some pretty rough looking penmanship that's sometimes barely legible. Guests will undoubtedly have trouble reading the signatures which will prompt them to ask the other guests what the hell they just wrote, thereby getting people engaged in conversations. And that's the point of this exercise. The first person to get all the guests' signatures wins a small prize.

FOUR LETTER WORD SEARCH

"Boob, I told you not to use those words."

FOUR LETTER WORD SEARCH

Before the party, write individual letters on sheets of paper and hand one to each guest. Guests pin or stick the letters to their chests and then try to pair up with other players to make a word. Four letter words are allowed - in fact they're encouraged. The group to create the most inventive (or most crude) word wins. (All words must be real...can't make up words like you do in *Scrabble*®.)

Bubble
TROUBLE

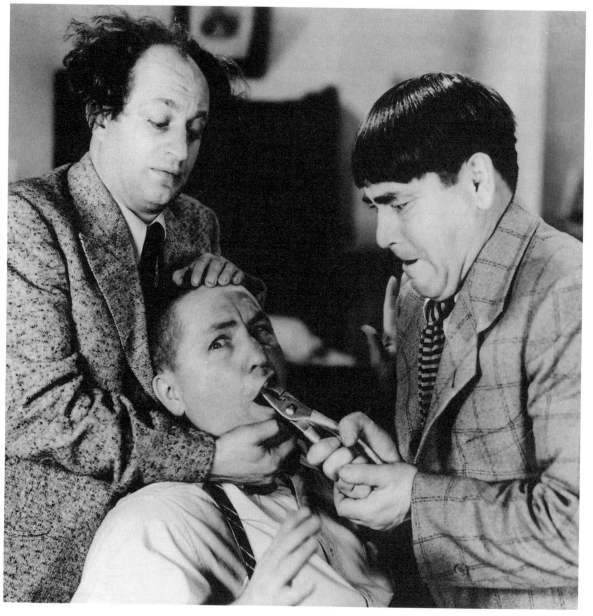

"Hold still knucklehead while I get the gum off your tonsils."

Bubble TROUBLE

Let's face it, we're all kids at heart. Who wouldn't love an excuse to chew giant wads of bubble gum and blow obnoxiously large bubbles.

Every player gets the same amount of gum which they chew until the wad reaches their favorite glumpy consistency for bubble blowing. Then they simply blow their brains out. The Judge determines who has blown the biggest bubble by carefully manipulating a ruler or something. Naturally, the person who blows the biggest bubble wins a prize and gets to use the mirrors first to pick the gum off their face and hair.

SiGNiFiCANT OTHER

Don't shoot Curly. He's half shot already.

SIGNIFICANT OTHER

Divide your coupled guests and direct the men go off into a separate room (that should be easy to accomplish – just point them toward the room with the bar.) Give the men a questionnaire to fill out with questions such as, What's your favorite color? Biggest pet peeve? Most annoying habit? Favorite flavor of ice cream? Favorite movie? First thing you do in morning?, etc.

"THINK, HARVEY, THINK."

When they finish filling in the blanks, collect their questionnaires and have them come back into the room to sit with their respective partners. Then ask each woman the same questions out loud. She answers with the responses she expects her partner to give and the couple with the lowest number of matching answers gets to shoot each other.

HUMAN DOMINOES

"Hey Moe. Hey Larry. Whaddaya doing lying on the floor?"

HUMAN DOMINOES

This is a good game for people who like to lie around on floors a lot and do touchy-feely activities. At a time during the party when the guests have had a few drinks and everyone is pretty familiar with each other, hand out pieces of paper with a domino piece drawn on it large enough to cover a player's chest. One person starts by lying on the floor and then, hopefully in man-woman order, other guests lie on top of each other following the rules of putting together the matching domino pieces.

What's the point of this game? Who knows and who cares? It's just a fun, physical activity that allows guests to get to know each other a little more intimately. There's no need for a winner because someone is going to come out on top regardless.

CHEEK TO CHEEK

We like this game a lot. Well, maybe Curly don't like it so good.

CHEEK TO CHEEK

If you liked Spin the Bottle as a kid, you're going to love this game. It's a fun, adult variation of Musical Chairs.

Players pair up and form two circles, one inside the other, and stand facing each other. Someone is selected as the Leader and another player is in charge of starting and stopping the music. As soon as the music starts, the two circles move in opposite directions. The Leader stands in the middle of the two circles and issues commands such as "head to head," "cheek to cheek," "elbow to knee," etc. When the music stops, players opposite each other must pair up their designated body part to that of their partner. (By the way, this game can be as tame or as wild as your gang will allow...) The Leader finds a player to pair up with when the music stops too and the "odd person out" becomes the next Leader. There may be no winner, but then again there is no loser either.

SELF PORTRAITS

When you see what these photos look like you may want to cut off a few of your own heads.

SELF PORTRAITS

This game is a cute, mindless exercise for guests to get to know each other better. Come to think of it, most of our games are pretty mindless. But, hey, you bought the book.

All you have to do is provide each guest with an unlined piece of paper and pencil, then explain that everyone is to draw a self-portrait – with the lights OFF. After everyone has mutilated their image of themselves on the paper, turn the lights back on and collect the drawings. As you hold each one up for all the group to see, guests try to match up the portraits to the names and faces at the party. *Don't let guests lean on your coffee tables to draw in the dark; you'll end up with scratches all over your furniture.*

NAME US FAMOUS

"All us famous people are pretty good looking, n'yuk, n'yuk, n'yuk."

NAME US FAMOUS

This one is an old favorite. Before the party, write the names of celebrities on separate pieces of paper. As guests arrive, tape one of these "name tags" to each person's back. Guests have no idea whom they are supposed to be, but they can see the names taped to the other players' backs. All participants must speak to each other as if they were addressing the real celebrities. The object of the game is for guests to figure out who they are by the tone in which they are addressed and by asking indirect questions about their identity. The game continues until every guest has guessed their celebrity status. Of course, if everyone at your party IS a celebrity, you can use name tags of street people, and indigenous bums like Typhus Annie or Colombian Carlos.

TALL TALE

When you win the *Tall Tale* Game you get to go first at the buffet table.

TALL TALE

Divide the guests into as many groups of four or six people as possible and hand each group a bag with five unrelated articles in it. The object of this thinking game is for the group to fabricate a story tying all five objects together. Each group has a time limit of two minutes to prepare their story so that most of it is really just ad-libbed. You can appoint a panel of judges to decide which group's story is the best based on creativity and humor, and that group wins a prize like being allowed to go first for the dessert buffet.

"HAD A SCIENTIFIC EXPERIMENT GONE TERRIBLY WRONG..."

OTHER GREAT BOOKS BY BOSTON AMERICA

The fine, cultivated stores carrying our books really get ticked if you buy directly from the publisher so if you can, please patronize your local store and let them make a buck. If, however, the fools don't carry a particular title, you can order them from us for $7, postpaid. Credit cards accepted for orders of 4 or more books.

#2400 How To Have Sex On Your Birthday
Finding a partner, special birthday sex positions, kinky sex and much more

#2403 The Good Bonking Guide
Bonking is a very useful British term for "you know what" and this book covers bonking in the dark, bonking all night long, improving your bonking and everything else you might want to know.

#2419 Cucumbers Are Better Than Men Because...
Cucumbers never go soft in a second, aren't afraid of commitment and never criticize.

#2423 Is There Sex After 40
It says normal couples do **it** at least once a week, you get the urge but can't remember what for and "if he was rigid I wouldn't be frigid".

#2424 Is There Sex After 50
Swapping him for two 25 year olds, being into gardening, wine making and group sex and liking it better when the bulge was in his trousers.

#2430 Is There Sex After 30
Being too tired to get it up, thinking kinky is leaving the lights on and remembering when you could do it 3 times a night.

#2432 Big Weenies
Big weenies and small weenies and all their names and how to find big weenies in a strange town and how to rate them.

#2434 Sex and Marriage
Wives wanting foreplay and romance and husbands wanting to be allowed to go to sleep right after. Techniques for improving your wife or husband or ignoring them.

#2438 Dog Farts
Dogs get blames for lots of farts they don't do but this book gives all the real ones like the sleeping dog fart and the living room fart.

#2446 The PMS Book
This book covers all the problems from irritability to clumsiness to chocolate craving to backaches in a funny and sympathetic manner.

#2450 How To Pick Up Girls
This book holds the keys to understanding women and teaches never fail lines plus places to meet shy, drunk weird and even naked girls

#2451 How To Pick Up Guys
How to get them to grovel at your feet and how to spot the losers and how to get rid of them after sex.

#2453 Beginners Sex Manual
Covers basics such as how to tell if you're a virgin and good things to say before and after sex.

#2455 Unspeakably Rotten Cartoons
Words cannot describe this totally tasteless and crass collection of cartoons that are guaranteed to offend and make you laugh.

#2457 Hooters
This is a photo book of the latest lingo for boobs and bosoms and bulging breasts.

#2458 Adult Connect The Dots
If you can count and use a pencil at the same time you too can be a pornographer.

#2463 Butts and Buns
These photos take a racy, rear view at women's tushes, beautiful buns and delicate derrieres.

#2465 Do It Yourself Guide To Safe Sex
Well if you do it yourself you can get it right the first time and never catch any nasty diseases.

#2466 Guide To Intimate Apparel
Photos and purposes of all the lacy lingerie and unmentionables from bloomers to garters to wedgies.

#2469 Hunks
A list of all the popular men's names and how they compare in bed and boardroom and physical sizes,

#2470 How To Find A Man And Get Married In 30 Days
Reserve the hall first and then learn ways and places to meet men, how to use sex and how to get rid of your mistakes,

#2471 Student Guide To Farting
The roommate fart, the math teacher fart, the lunch lady fart. This book covers them all.

#2472 Party Games For 30 Year Olds
New racy games and lists of old favorites. This book has them all and will keep a party of 30 year olds going all night.

#2473 Party Games For 40 Year Olds
Similar to the 30 year old book with perhaps more emphasis on sex rather than drinking.

#2474 Party Games For 50 Year Olds
Just like the 30 and 40 year old games but this book gives instruction on keeping the players awake after 10 PM

#2501 Cowards Guide To Body Piercing
Cartoons and explanations of all the good and horrible places you can put holes in yourself.

#2502 Toilet Tips
Urinal etiquette and handling warm toilet seats or doors with lousy locks or smells that are not your own. A must for anyone that uses toilets.

#2503 Kinky World Records
Like the world's hairiest armpits or thickest condom or shortest male organ or longest time to take off a bra. Hey, you could set your own records.

#2504 Pregnant Woman's Guide To Farting
The Claustrophobia Fart and the Waiting Room Fart and the Naming the Baby Fart and the Constipation Fart are just a few.

#2505 Is There Sex After Retirement
Cartoons for the retired set such as, "If he was rigid I wouldn't b frigid" and "Of course I'll respect you in the morning you blind old bat. I'm your husband.

#2506 Farting Under The Covers And Other Secrets Of Successful Marriage.
Secret things husbands and wives do, secrets of regularity and secrets of listening to your wife.

#2700 Rules For Sex On Your Wedding Night
Rules for sex on the way to the hotel and rules for keeping up your energy and rules for couples who have been living together for 2 years.

#2701 Dictionary Of Doodie
Feels Like Shit, Shit Head, Shit On A Shingle, Shit Talk and all the other colorful uses of this most important word in the English language.

#2702 Alien Doodle Book
Doodle in all your favorite Aliens in ridiculous sexual escapades with humans.

#2703 You Know Your A Golf Addict When....
When you hustle your grandma, watch golf videos and think you look attractive in golf clothes.

#2704 What Every Woman Can Learn From Her Cat
An unmade bed is fluffier, there's no problem that can't be helped by a nap and when you want a little attention, roll over on your back.

#2705 Adult Connect The Dots
If you can count from 1 to 100 you can be a pornographer. You won't believe the results of your creativity

#1100 The 3 Stooges Book Of Party Games
You want to have a good party? Soitenly. So grab a few games from this riotous book.

125 Walnut Street
Watertown, MA 02172
(617) 923-1111   FAX: (617) 923-8839

BOSTON AMERICA
C★O★R★P